W9-AVM-124

cool science

Astrobiology

Fred Bortz

LERNER PUBLICATIONS COMPANY
MINNEAPOLIS

To the first Earthlings on Mars,
who may be reading this book.
Are you one of them?

Lerner Publications Company
A division of Lerner Publishing Group, Inc.
241 First Avenue North
Minneapolis, MN 55401 U.S.A.

Website address: www.lernerbooks.com

Library of Congress Cataloging-in-Publication Data

Bortz, Alfred B.
Astrobiology / by Fred Bortz.
p. cm. — (Cool science)
Includes bibliographical references and index.
ISBN-13: 978-0-8225-6771-4 (lib. bdg. : alk. paper)
1. Space biology—Juvenile literature. 2. Life on other planets—Juvenile literature. I. Title.
QH327.B67 2008
571.0919—dc22 2006033268

Manufactured in the United States of America
1 2 3 4 5 6 - JR - 13 12 11 10 09 08

Table of Contents

Introduction

Here's a new version of an old story. Once upon a time, an alien named Goldilocks went for a ride in the Milky Way Galaxy. The Milky Way is the star system that includes our solar system. Goldilocks passed star clusters and nebulas. She dodged pulsars, supernovas, and black holes looking for a good place to land. She didn't stop at Betelgeuse and Antares because those stars were too red. She zipped by Sirius and Rigel—they were too blue. Then she saw the bright yellow Sun of our solar system.

Goldilocks decided to stop at one of the planets around the Sun, refuel her rocket, and have a picnic. When she got to Venus and passed through its clouds, she had to turn back. This second planet from the Sun was so hot that Goldilocks's spacecraft almost melted.

Then she flew out to Mars, the fourth planet from the Sun. But its air was too cold and thin. Its surface was a cratered, rocky desert. No good for a picnic!

So she zoomed back around planet Earth, the third planet from the Sun. It was not too hot and not too cold. She could breathe its air, and the sunlight was perfect. She saw clouds, oceans, and land filled with plants and animals. It was just right! Goldilocks landed her spacecraft and settled down with her picnic basket.

Yes, our Earth is such a perfect place for life that some astrobiologists call it a Goldilocks planet. Astrobiologists are scientists who study life in the universe. The name of their science is a combination of *biology* (the study of life) and *astronomy* (the study of the stars, the planets, and other bodies of our solar system).

Earth's combination of water, air, and plants make it just right for life.

Astrobiology is an unusual science, because it is the study of something that may not exist. No one knows for certain whether life exists beyond Earth. But astrobiologists have plenty of reasons to suspect that it does. They think about alien life-forms in our solar system and even other solar systems! They ask themselves how those life-forms might be like or unlike living things on Earth. Some even ask if there might be aliens such as Goldilocks, smart and skillful enough to be looking for planets like their own.

IT'S A FACT!

Astrobiology began as exobiology, the study of life beyond our planet. (*Exo* is Greek for "outside.") To understand life on other worlds, we have to start with life on Earth. So the science became the study of life anywhere in the universe, and its name changed to astrobiology.

chapter 1

Lunar Beginnings

Astrobiology is a new science, but it has ancient roots. Past civilizations could see the Sun and the Moon. They could also see the five planets we call Mercury, Venus, Mars, Jupiter, and Saturn. People in ancient times noticed patterns in the daily, monthly, and yearly movements of the Sun and Moon. They noted the motion of the five planets as they wandered across the background of the stars.

This ancient Egyptian painting shows the star-filled sky as the body of the goddess Nut. She stretches over Shu, the air god (*center*), and Geb, the earth god (*bottom*).

Ancient people's study of the heavens was more like religion than science. They thought of the planets as gods as well as heavenly bodies. They carefully observed and recorded the planets' colors and movements. But they did not have any instruments to see details about the planets. Ancient people simply didn't know enough about the planets to imagine them as worlds of their own.

Life on the Moon?

The Moon, however, was different. It was close enough to inspire the human imagination.

About 1,900 years ago, the Greek scholar Plutarch observed the features of the Moon. He interpreted what he saw as mountains, plains, and seas. He even imagined humanlike beings that might live there.

We know that Plutarch was wrong about life on the Moon. But a wrong answer can sometimes lead people in a useful direction. Plutarch was one of the first to ask two very important questions. Is there life on other worlds? And if so, in what ways is that life similar to or different from Earth's? People still ask those questions. They are the main questions of astrobiology.

IT'S A FACT!

Plutarch imagined that Moon dwellers might gaze down on Earth and wonder if it could support life like theirs. But Plutarch was wrong that Moon beings would look *down*. Astronauts walked on the Moon during missions from 1969 to 1972. They had to look upward—in the direction opposite the Moon's gravity—to see their home planet.

Early Greeks linked the Moon (*below*) with the goddess Artemis. But by Plutarch's time, the Greeks knew the Moon was a body going around Earth.

How Earth and the Moon are Similar (and Different)

Plutarch thought Earth and the Moon were very similar and might have similar life. We know now that the two worlds are very different. Earth has air and bodies of water such as rivers and oceans. The Moon has neither. At its center, Earth has a heavy core of molten metal. Floating on that are two layers of rock called the mantle and the crust. The Moon is too lightweight to have a metal core. It seems to be all rock.

Yet modern scientists suspected that Earth and the Moon formed in a similar way from similar substances. But they couldn't know for sure until astronauts collected rocks from the Moon's surface between 1969 and 1972. Scientists found that the Moon minerals were almost identical, atom for atom, to Earth minerals. Earth's crust and mantle and the Moon must have formed from the same event!

What could that event have been? Scientists thought of many possibilities. They then came to a conclusion. In its earliest history, Earth collided with a planet about the size of Mars. During the collision, the other planet's heavy core probably became part of Earth's. Lighter rock from both planets sprayed into orbit. Gravity pulled those orbiting fragments together, forming the Moon.

After the collision, Earth was left with everything needed for life, including water and air. But the Moon became a lifeless world.

What the Telescope Tells

In 1609 Italian scientist Galileo Galilei heard about a new Dutch invention called the telescope. He decided to build one for himself. Most people then used their telescopes to magnify distant objects on Earth. But Galileo turned his toward the sky. Seeing the Moon's craters and measuring the height of its mountains was exciting. But his greatest discovery came when he looked at Jupiter early in 1610. He saw four points of light near the planet. They changed their position nightly. He realized he was seeing moons traveling around Jupiter just as the Moon orbits Earth.

In Galileo's time, most people believed that Earth was the center of the universe. They believed that everything in the heavens—the Sun, stars, other planets—circled around Earth. But scientists thought differently. They realized that Earth and the other five planets traveled around the Sun. Jupiter's moons showed that the scientists were on the right track. Not every object in the sky circled Earth.

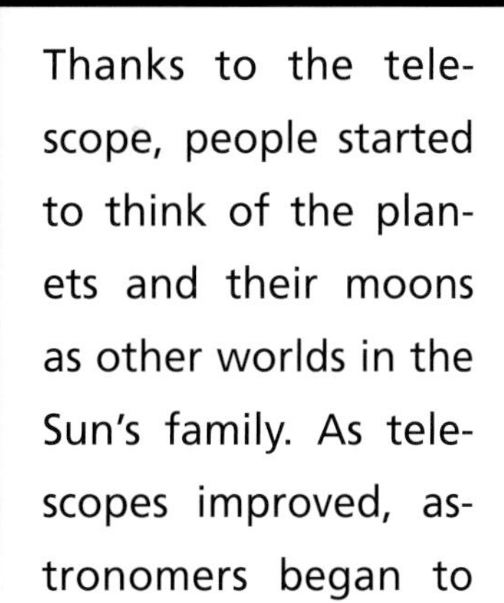

In 1633 the powerful Roman Catholic Church put Galileo (*right* and *below, center left*) on trial for publishing his astronomy theories. The idea of a Sun-centered universe went against religious beliefs of the time.

Thanks to the telescope, people started to think of the planets and their moons as other worlds in the Sun's family. As telescopes improved, astronomers began to see more details on those worlds. They saw colored bands and swirls on Jupiter. They saw Saturn's rings.

Of course, Venus and Mars, the two planets closest to Earth, drew much attention. Venus was bright in the sky. But its atmosphere was thick with clouds. Not even the best telescopes could see past the clouds to any details of the planet's surface.

Mars was much more interesting. It was like Earth in some very important ways. Astronomers using telescopes saw ice around Mars's north and south poles. They watched those polar ice caps shrink in the summer and grow in winter, as the ice around Earth's North Pole does. And parts of the Martian surface darkened with the coming of spring. Astronomers wondered, Could that be vegetation, or plant life?

Details of the surface of Mars (*above*) were easily seen through early telescopes.

Lunar Cities and Martian Canals

As astronomers saw more features on the surfaces of the Moon and Mars, they began to draw detailed maps. The English astronomer William Herschel (1738–1822) built the greatest telescopes of his time. In 1776 he claimed to see large areas of vegetation on the Moon. This vegetation, he claimed, included forests of trees four to six times taller than Earth's trees.

Herschel went beyond observing the Moon. He got carried away with other ideas. He wrote about lunar lawns and pastures. He even went so far as to imagine the Moon's craters as walled cities built by Lunarians (Moon dwellers).

Herschel had some wild ideas about the Moon. One was that Lunarians were half human, half bat (*below*).

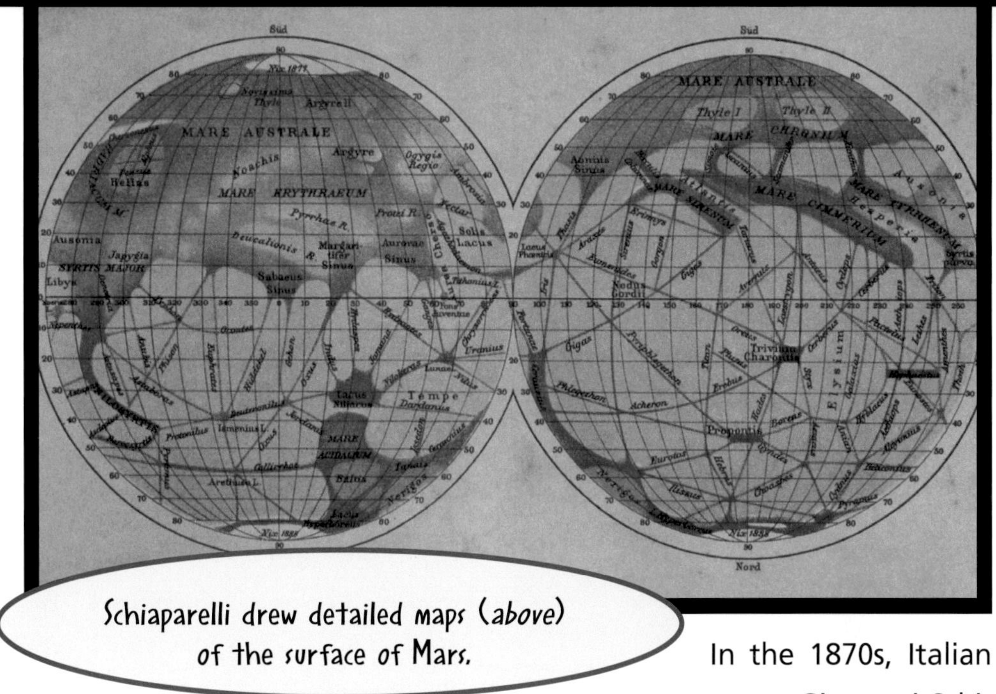

Schiaparelli drew detailed maps (above) of the surface of Mars.

In the 1870s, Italian astronomer Giovanni Schiaparelli decided that it was time to improve the maps of Mars. Until then, Martian maps had only large, vague areas. Schiaparelli's new maps included sharper features. They included lines he called *canali*. *Canali* is Italian for "channels."

Many English-speaking astronomers translated that word as "canals." The difference between channels and canals is important. Channels can form naturally. But only intelligent beings (beings that can think and plan) can build canals.

Among the astronomers who took up the term *canals* was Percival Lowell. Lowell came from a wealthy American family of writers and scholars. He used his fortune to build a large astronomical observatory (a building equipped to study the planets

IT'S A FACT!

Percival Lowell built an observatory to study Mars. Its location became known as Mars Hill.

Percival Lowell (*above*) spent twenty-three years studying Mars.

and stars) in Flagstaff, Arizona. Lowell wanted to focus his studies on Mars.

Lowell spent years observing Mars. He made drawings of what he saw on Mars through his telescopes. He gave public talks about what he saw. He also wrote popular books. His 1895 book *Mars* described a planet older than Earth. An intelligent civilization, he claimed, lived (or had once lived) on the planet.

Lowell had an idea about the canals on Mars. Mars was becoming a desert, he wrote. It was getting hotter and drier. Martians needed a way to bring water from melting polar ice to their cities. So, Martian engineers had built the canals to carry the water. It was a fascinating story. But it was wrong.

chapter 2

Speculation and Observation

Herschel's Lunarians and Lowell's Martians did not come from actual sightings and study of those beings. They were speculation. Speculation is a fancy name for making a leap in thinking without much solid information. Speculation can be creative and can lead science in new directions. But sometimes scientists want so badly for their ideas to be correct that they misread evidence. Speculating scientists need to be careful of wishful thinking.

Herschel, Lowell, and many others liked to speculate about life on other planets. They also hoped to be the first to discover that life. That's a natural human ambition. Another natural human way of thinking is to assume that life on other worlds is like life on Earth.

Astrobiologists fight against those natural inclinations. They look at images from other planets and see signs of life. But they force themselves to look first for other explanations. Modern astrobiologists still do plenty of speculating. They think about the possibility of all kinds of alien life. But they always ask certain questions. What is the evidence? Are there other ways to interpret it? And what else do we need to know?

Mars Up Close

New advances in scientific instruments help scientists weed out wishful thinking. But sometimes those advances happen slowly. For example, in 1907 the first photographs of Mars taken through Lowell's telescopes became available. The images were not clear. Scientists knew they needed to know more. They wanted to explore Mars up close. But they didn't get their chance until the early 1960s.

The War of the Worlds

In the late 1800s, speculation about intelligent Martians led science-fiction writer H. G. Wells to some interesting questions. What if Martians turned out to be smarter and more advanced than humans? And what if they weren't friendly? Would Martians use their knowledge of space travel and weaponry to invade Earth?

The result was Wells's classic novel, *The War of the Worlds*, published in 1898. Wells's book remained popular. On October 30, 1938, a radio broadcast of *The War of the Worlds* caused panic across the United States. At the beginning of the show, an announcer explained that the story was fiction. But the rest of the show had realistic-sounding news bulletins and reports. Many listeners who tuned in late thought a Martian invasion was actually under way in New Jersey. Since then several movie versions of *The War of the Worlds* have been made. Steven Spielberg directed one in 2005.

In those years, the United States and the Soviet Union came close to going to war. Both countries raced to develop military technology. Some of this new technology also helped to explore the Moon and other planets. In 1964 the U.S. National Aeronautics and Space Administration (NASA) launched the Mariner 4 mission to Mars. *Mariner 4* flew by Mars and returned twenty-one images. They showed a dry, cratered surface that looked more like the Moon than Earth.

IT'S A FACT!

Mariner 4 was the second attempted U.S. mission to Mars. The Soviet Union had launched five earlier spacecraft toward Mars, with one near success. Its *Mars 1* flew by the planet in June 1963. But it lost radio contact about halfway to Mars.

Space mission discoveries ruled out intelligent life on Mars's surface. But did it end hope of finding any living creatures there? In 1975 two U.S. Viking missions landed on Mars to gather more information. The *Viking* craft returned close-up images from the planet's surface. The craft also took samples of the soil and the atmosphere. It tested the samples with onboard instruments.

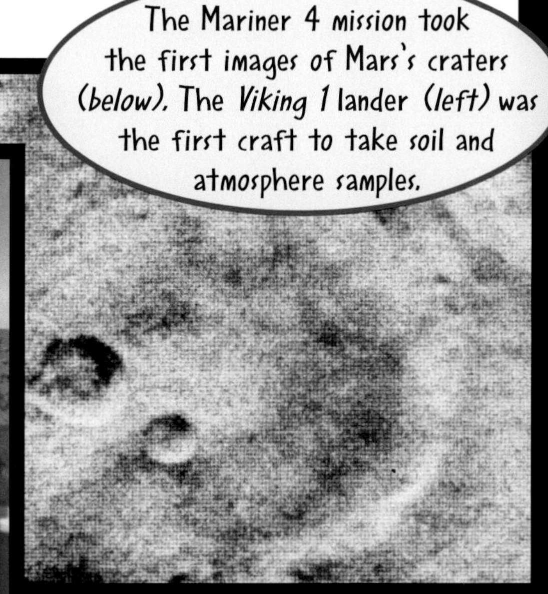

The Mariner 4 mission took the first images of Mars's craters (below). The *Viking 1* lander (left) was the first craft to take soil and atmosphere samples.

Those instruments told NASA scientists that Mars could not support plant or animal life. Its atmosphere is too thin, with little oxygen and water. But tests of the soil samples seemed at first to show signs of bacteria (microscopic, single-cell organisms). Scientists were excited. But they knew they had to look for other explanations. Soon they came up with a different explanation that did not involve bacteria.

Mars on Earth

With no clear signs of life on Mars, the exploration program slowed. But it did not end. The test results from the Mars samples gave scientists plenty to think about. The samples of the atmosphere were very useful to people who studied meteorites (rocks from outer space that fall to Earth).

These scientists compared the gases trapped in the meteorites to the samples of Mars's atmosphere. They found that a handful of meteorites contained gas that matched the Martian atmosphere. This told planetary scientists that the meteorites might have come from Mars. Even without another mission to Mars, scientists could study space-traveling bits of the planet. One Martian meteorite, the size and shape of a baking potato, was very fascinating. Called ALH84001, it was found in the Allan Hills area of Antarctica in 1984.

When found, meteorite ALH84001 was 6 x 4 x 3 inches (15 x 10 x 7 centimeters) and weighed almost 5 pounds (2 kilograms).

The Antarctic Search for Meteorites Program

Meteorite ALH84001 is one of the most famous rocks in the world. Like most of the pieces of Mars on Earth, it was found in Antarctica. Why there of all places?

Meteorites can and do fall all over Earth. But it is easier to find them in Antarctica. Antarctica is covered with ice and snow. So the dark meteorites stand out against their surroundings. Also, the movement of the continent's ice sheets gathers rocks together and moves them along. That makes it easy to know where to look.

During the Antarctic summer of 1976–1977, scientists began the Antarctic Search for Meteorites Program (ANSMET). In this ongoing project, ANSMET scientists have collected more than ten thousand meteorites. Most are pieces of asteroids (large rocky bodies that orbit the Sun mainly in a belt between Mars and Jupiter). But some are pieces of the Moon or Mars.

Even among Martian meteorites, ALH84001 was unusual. It came from rock formed very early in Mars's history. The meteorite also contained mineral deposits that could only have been formed by flowing water. In 1996 NASA scientists found microscopic traces of chemicals and structures inside those deposits. The tiny structures looked like those formed by bacteria on Earth.

Was ALH84001 telling us that we could find signs of ancient Martian life right here on Earth? That question was an astrobiologist's dream!

chapter 3

Bringing Astrobiology Down to Earth

The NASA scientists studying Meteorite ALH84001 knew they would have a hard time convincing people of their findings. Would other scientists believe that they had seen signs of ancient Martian bacteria? In an article they wrote for the journal *Science*, the NASA scientists worded their discovery very carefully. They didn't claim they had found life on Mars. They only said that they had found four signs of life:

1. **A mixture of chemicals called polycyclic aromatic hydrocarbons (PAHs).** PAHs are produced by decaying organisms on Earth. But they can also form in other ways. The NASA scientists claimed that the mixture of PAHs in ALH84001 were like those produced by Earth life.

2. **Grains of a magnetic form of iron oxide known as magnetite.** The grains in ALH84001 were like magnetite grains produced by a kind of Earth bacteria.

3. **Grains of a form of iron sulfide known as greigite.** The grains of greigite in ALH84001 are shaped like greigite at the core of certain Earth bacteria. They are smaller, though.

4. **Microscopic structures within the meteorite.** The structures look like smaller versions of fossils left behind by bacteria on Earth.

Scientists discovered what looked like bacteria fossils (above and right) inside ALH84001.

Every one of the four signs has one thing in common. The scientists were comparing the evidence in ALH84001 to life on Earth.

As expected, other scientists doubted the signs of ancient Martian life. Soon only the original research team and a few others stuck to the claims. Still, everyone agreed that comparing the ALH84001 evidence to Earth life was important. The best way to understand life on Mars—or on any other world—is to start by understanding how life began and evolved on Earth.

Recipes for Life

It takes a Goldilocks planet to support complex life-forms such as flowers, trees, fish, birds, bugs, and animals. But microbes (simple, microscopic organisms) such as bacteria can get by on much less. Astrobiologists began asking if any kind of life could survive on a non-Goldilocks planet such as Mars.

Extremophiles

Even our Goldilocks planet Earth has places where humans and the usual types of animals cannot survive. Earth has extremely cold and extremely hot regions. It has bodies of water filled with salt or harsh acids, and mountaintops where the air is thin. Can simpler life-forms develop and thrive in these extreme surroundings? Scientists have found that the answer is yes.

Extremophiles—creatures that thrive in extreme conditions—have been found in many places on Earth. Some extremophile bacteria live near mineral-rich streams of hot water that rise from the ocean floor. Some live in bedrock miles beneath the Earth. And some live in very cold and salty lakes beneath the ice of Antarctica.

These extremophile bacteria (*above*) thrive in hydrothermal (hot water) vents on the ocean floor.

These extremophile bacteria (*right*) thrive in very hot saltwater puddles.

Those Antarctic extremophiles could survive on Mars. They make astrobiologists wonder if similar life-forms could have evolved on Mars. And if they evolved there, do they have living descendants?

To investigate that idea, astrobiologists start by looking at the beginning of life on Earth. If they understand the recipe for life on Earth, then they will know what to look for on other worlds.

A recipe has two important sections. The first is a list of ingredients. The second is a series of steps to turn those ingredients into a tasty and nutritious dish. On Earth all forms of life have one ingredient in common—a large, complex molecule called deoxyribonucleic acid (DNA).

But DNA is not just an ingredient. It is also the cookbook. Each molecule of DNA in a living organism contains all the instructions for creating that organism. And that includes making more DNA molecules. The secret is in the way the atoms of a DNA molecule are put together.

The DNA molecule is shaped like a spiral staircase with a left-handed, or clockwise, spiral. The DNA staircase is called a double helix. Each helix is made of alternating sugar and phosphate molecules connected by oxygen atoms. Together, the two helixes form a strong pair of staircase railings.

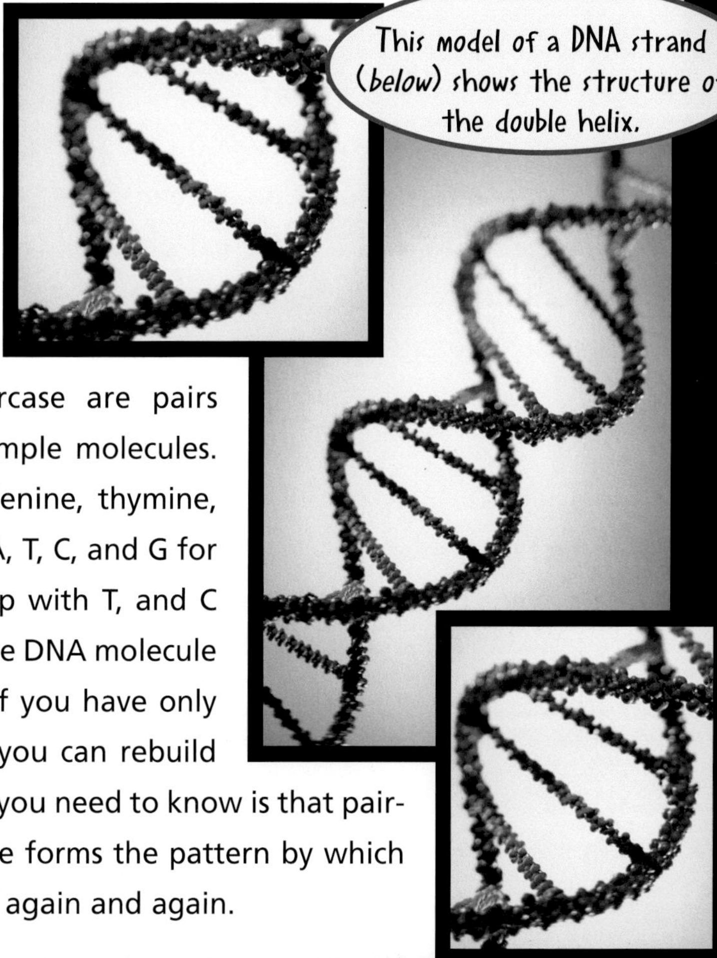

This model of a DNA strand (*below*) shows the structure of the double helix.

The steps of the staircase are pairs (called base pairs) of simple molecules. Those molecules are adenine, thymine, cytosine, and guanine (A, T, C, and G for short). A always pairs up with T, and C with G. The pairs hold the DNA molecule together like a zipper. If you have only one-half of the zipper, you can rebuild the whole molecule. All you need to know is that pairing rule. The pairing rule forms the pattern by which DNA can duplicate itself again and again.

More than DNA

Duplication explains why there can be large numbers of one kind of DNA molecule. But if DNA is always duplicating itself, where do all the different kinds of DNA come from? How does DNA lead to so many different Earth life-forms?

That's where the recipe's instructions come in. The arrangement of the A, T, C, and G molecules on the stairway is called the genetic code. The code is a step-by-step guide to putting together small molecules called amino acids. The amino acids build larger molecules called proteins. Proteins are very important for forming body organs or plant parts. For this reason, amino acids are considered the building blocks of life. Nature allows for many amino acids. But for some reason, the genetic code of Earth life has chosen only twenty.

Different sequences of pairs along the DNA staircase produce different genetic codes. The codes produce different sets of proteins. Different sets of proteins lead to different organisms. Sometimes, DNA duplication isn't perfect. The "daughter" DNA molecule is a little different from the "parent." That difference is called a mutation.

Mutations are, in a way, experiments in which Nature creates new DNA molecules at random. Most of the experiments are failures. They often produce an unhealthy mutation. That mutant organism and its DNA do not survive. But some other mutations are successful. Organisms carrying a successful mutation can reproduce and pass along the new DNA.

Evolution

Mutation is a step in a process known as evolution. From studying Earth life, astrobiologists realize that even the simplest life-forms anywhere must be able to evolve. Evolution starts when a mutation leads to an organism with a new or improved ability. That mutated organism may survive better in certain environments. So it may survive in one area while its normal cousins survive elsewhere.

IT'S A FACT!

Protein molecules do their work by folding up into particular shapes. If a mutation changes the protein, it may also change that shape. Just as a jigsaw puzzle piece from the wrong box usually ruins a puzzle's picture, the mutant protein usually leads to an organ or body process that doesn't work.

Some organisms may not survive in new environments. Evolution means that a few of those organisms' many descendants may be lucky to evolve in just the right way. Their different DNA gives them just the right characteristics to live on while other organisms die off.

On the Goldilocks planet Earth, evolution has produced many complex life-forms, including humans. Evolution is a very slow process. It depends on random changes in a DNA molecule. Most of those changes do not survive. To produce so many different kinds of living organisms, Earth has had to be a Goldilocks planet for a very long time.

Besides DNA, what else makes Earth suitable for life and evolution? Every organism on the planet needs liquid water. Water makes life's chemistry possible. It dissolves many different substances and brings them together. That means life can't exist in places that are so hot that all the water boils off. It can't exist in places that are so cold that all the water freezes. Most organisms on Earth also need gases such as oxygen from the atmosphere. Even ocean life must have atmospheric gases dissolved in the water.

Life also needs energy to make its chemistry work. For example, green plants capture the energy in sunlight. Animals get energy from eating plants or other animals. But some unusual life-forms draw their energy from other sources, such as the Earth's inner heat.

Is life based on water and DNA the only kind that can exist on other worlds? Astrobiologists like to think about that question. They also wonder about what it took to get life started on Earth. Where did the first amino acids and DNA molecules come from? Does life start up easily if all the chemicals to make DNA are in one place? Or did something unusual happen on Earth to make them combine?

If our space-traveling Goldilocks were an astrobiologist, she would realize that she couldn't answer those questions by studying just one planet. After studying life on Earth, she'd be off to explore the rest of the solar system for evidence of life. Her next destination would probably be Mars.

IT'S A FACT!

Earth's early atmosphere had almost no oxygen. Then primitive plant life evolved photosynthesis. Through photosynthesis, plants capture energy from the Sun. The energy helps plants combine water with a gas called carbon dioxide to make sugar for food and to release oxygen.

chapter 4

Life in the Solar System

Why is Mars the first place most astrobiologists look for life beyond Earth? Why not the Moon? The Moon is much closer and easier to explore. Its rocks resemble Earth's. But the Moon never had an atmosphere or liquid water. Without air or water, life could not develop. The Moon is a great place for collecting rocks but not for finding signs of life.

What about Venus? It is a near twin to our planet in size and chemical makeup. The problem is its temperature. The surface of Venus is almost 900°F (480°C). That's hot enough to melt many metals. It's far too hot for liquid water. In its early history,

IT'S A FACT!

The Moon has no wind or flowing water, so its rocks hardly change. It has meteorites from the young solar system—including bits of Mercury, Venus, Mars, and especially Earth. These bits lie unchanged where they landed. Astrobiologists who want to study Earth's oldest rocks may find them on the Moon.

Venus was probably cool enough to have rivers and oceans. Earthlike life-forms might have evolved there. But because of the extreme heat, it's not possible to explore the planet. No spacecraft would last long enough to search for evidence of Venus's past life.

IT'S A FACT!

If Venus currently has life anywhere, it would be acid-loving extremophiles floating in its clouds. It would be hard enough to detect organisms like that on Earth. Imagine trying to find them on another world!

Much of Venus's thick cloud layer is droplets of sulfuric acid, a strong and (to humans) poisonous chemical.

Looking for Life on Mars

Exploring Mars is much easier. Chemically, it is a lot like Earth. But it is much smaller—about half as big around and one-tenth as heavy. It has a thin atmosphere and icy polar caps. On the surface near its equator, Mars occasionally gets warm enough for liquid water. Sometimes, underground water bursts up to create a Martian stream. The Mars Global Surveyor satellite has captured images of Martian gullies—trenches where water had flowed.

But any water on the surface of Mars evaporates very quickly. A more likely place to find liquid water on Mars is below its surface. In fact, astrobiologists are already studying Martian meteorites. They are examining the rocks for signs of water and simple organisms from the past or present.

Water creates gullies (*below*) on the surface of Mars.

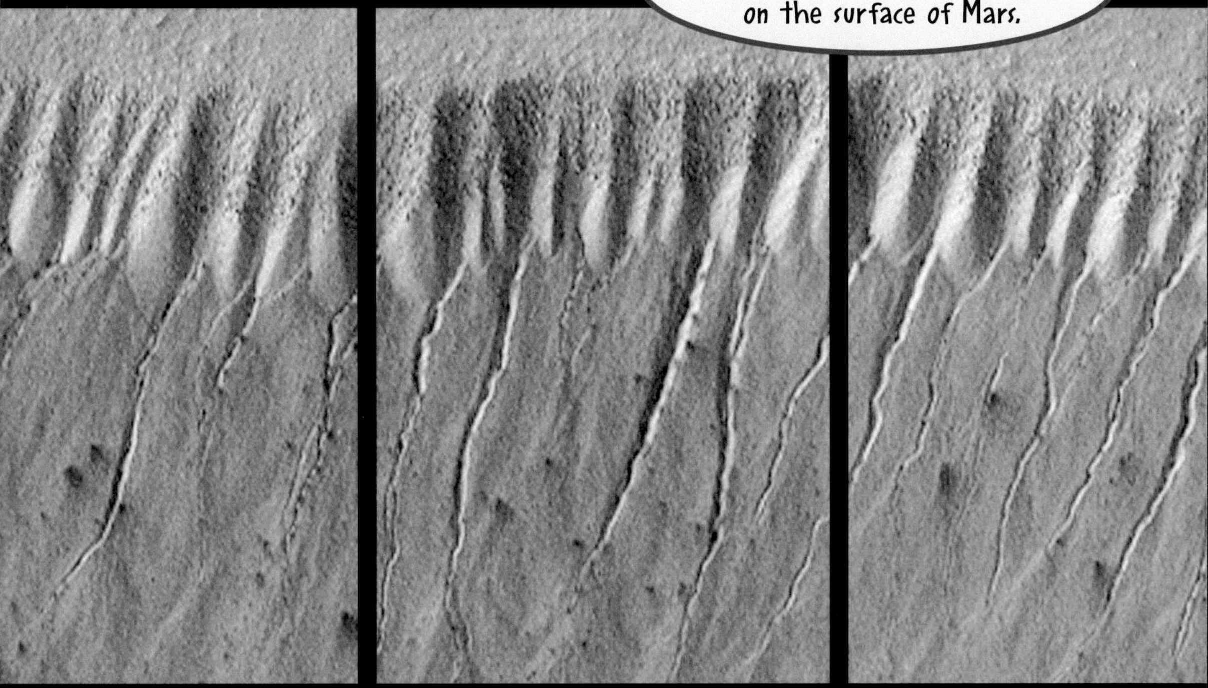

The scientists on the Viking missions of the 1970s asked the question, "Is there life on Mars now?" Since then, scientists have become more interested in another question, "Was there ever life on Mars?" To understand this new question, let's look at the discoveries in Meteorite ALH84001. We'll start with its formation on Mars long ago.

Early Earth and early Mars were quite similar. Very few of Earth's early rocks remain. Scientists can study them in only a few locations, such as in western Australia. They see signs that simple life-forms developed very quickly. That leads astrobiologists to a theory that simple life might also have begun on Mars. Its smaller size and greater distance from the Sun may have kept it from becoming an Earthlike Goldilocks planet for plants and animals. But for bacteria, Mars was just right—and may still be.

That is why Meteorite ALH84001 is so important to this story. Scientists have shown that the meteorite formed very early in Mars's history. They also know that it was exposed to flowing water and carbon dioxide gas. And they found four important signs of life—PAHs, magnetite grains, greigite grains, and possible bacteria "fossils."

If the meteorite had been an Earth rock rather than a piece of Mars, most scientists would reach a conclusion easily. They would look at this evidence and agree that bacteria had probably once lived inside the rock. We know there are bacteria—and all kinds of other life—on Earth. So the conclusion would be simple. But it would be quite a leap for scientists to conclude that the evidence in ALH84001 means Mars once had life. They need more convincing evidence than that.

For instance, it would be valuable to find places on Mars where the rocks have similar histories to ALH84001. We could then send rovers to collect local rocks and soil and return them to Earth. Eventually humans may land on Mars to look for signs of past or present life. If all goes as planned, the readers of this book will be just about the right age to be among those Mars explorers.

An artist's illustration of a NASA rover (*below, right*) explores the rocky surface of Mars (*below, left*).

The Mars explorers will have some big questions on their minds. How does life come from lifeless chemistry? Does life start wherever the right chemicals and sources of energy are in the right place? If the chemicals are Earthlike, will that life also be Earthlike? And how will they recognize signs of life, especially if it is different from the organisms on Earth?

Unearthly DNA?

When astrobiologists speculate about life on other planets, they usually think of organisms based on water and a molecule such as DNA. But if they ever find an alien life-form, one of the first things they will look for is a difference in its DNA and its proteins.

What differences might they find? The alien DNA might have other base pairs (not just A and T, C and G of Earth DNA). Slightly different amino acids might make up the organism's proteins (not just the twenty of Earth life). It is even possible for the alien DNA staircase to spiral in the opposite direction.

What if astrobiologists find alien DNA that is very different from Earth DNA? They might conclude that DNA's variety of ingredients and combinations are endless. But if the alien DNA is very similar to Earth DNA, an answer would be harder to find. Would it mean that DNA forms easily anywhere? And that something in nature always chooses the same twenty amino acids wherever that happens? Or would it mean that all the DNA in our solar system formed in one place? Did all DNA spread to different worlds on comets, asteroids, and bits of rock such as Meteorite ALH84001?

Which way makes more sense? That's a big question for astrobiologists. But until someone finds alien life, they will only be able to speculate about the answer.

Europa and Titan

In 1979 two Voyager spacecraft flew by Jupiter and changed astrobiology forever. Images of one of Jupiter's moons, Europa, showed that Europa's surface was covered in ice. When a moon is close to its planet, the gravitational pull between them is much stronger on their near sides than on their far sides. That difference in gravity causes tides on Earth's oceans, and so we call it a tidal force. Jupiter's powerful tidal force heats the interior of Europa enough to melt some of its ice. This melting ice combines with minerals to form a briny (salty) ocean beneath the ice crust. Scientists estimate that Europa's worldwide ocean is 30 miles (50 kilometers) deep. It lies beneath a 3-mile (5 km) crack-filled crust. A liquid ocean filled with minerals and a source of energy (heat) makes Europa a place where some form of life may exist.

The surface of Europa (*above*) is covered in cracks visible from space.

IT'S A FACT!

Between 1995 and 2003, a spacecraft named *Galileo* explored Jupiter and its moons. It discovered signs that the moons Ganymede and Callisto may also have underground oceans.

Finding an ocean on Europa changed astrobiologists' thinking about how close a world has to be to its sun to have life. More of Europa's energy comes from Jupiter's tidal forces than from the Sun. So if life is possible as far from the Sun as Jupiter, could there be life even farther away?

Could there be life, for example, on Saturn? That planet is nearly twice as far from the Sun as Jupiter and almost ten times as far from the Sun as Earth.

Astrobiologists are very interested in Saturn's largest moon, Titan. Titan is larger than the planet Mercury. It is the second-largest moon in our solar system. (Jupiter's Ganymede is slightly larger.) Titan's atmosphere and surface are both interesting for astrobiologists. Its thick atmosphere is more than 98 percent nitrogen, with 1.6 percent methane and small amounts of other gases. Titan's surface temperature is very cold—about –290°F (–179°C). At that temperature, water freezes as hard as a rock. Methane and ammonia, both gases on Earth, are liquid on Titan.

Interest in life on Titan grew during the Cassini mission. On July 1, 2004, the *Cassini* spacecraft went into orbit around Saturn to start a four-year exploration. *Cassini*'s orbit often takes it close to Titan and other moons. At every flyby, *Cassini* sends new images of those moons back to Earth. The most spectacular images of Titan were collected by *Huygens*,

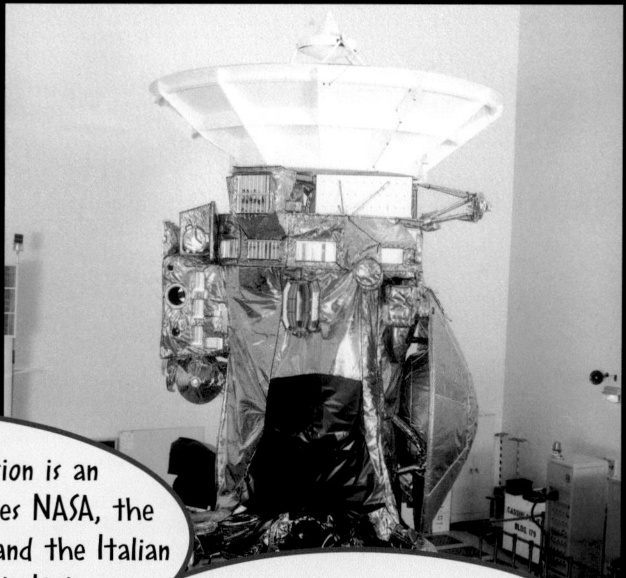

The *Cassini-Huygens* mission is an international effort. It involves NASA, the European Space Agency (ESA), and the Italian space agency, Agenzia Spaziale Italiana.

Every day, more than 250 scientists worldwide study the data sent back from the *Cassini* orbiter and the *Huygens* lander (*above*).

This photo of Titan (*above and right*) was made from sixteen separate images taken by the *Cassini* orbiter.

a small craft released by *Cassini* in late December 2004. In mid-January 2005, *Huygens* landed on Titan. *Huygens* took pictures during its descent and for ninety minutes afterward.

IT'S A FACT!

Some astrobiologists talk about life even farther from the Sun than Titan. Neptune's moon, Triton, is three times farther from the Sun than Titan. But those scientists speculate that it might also be suitable for silicon-based life.

The images showed a strangely Earthlike surface of rocks and dunes. There were also signs of flowing streams and possibly seas or lakes. Those surface features looked similar to bodies of water on Earth. But Titan's streams and lakes are most likely made up of ammonia, methane, ethane, and oily chemicals known as hydrocarbons.

Titan is a very active world. Its hydrocarbons probably come from volcanoes. Its thick atmosphere has unearthly weather, including methane rainstorms. Beneath its surface, it probably has oceans of water and ammonia. The combination of chemicals needed for life plus flowing gases and liquids makes it easy to imagine that extremophiles could thrive there.

Some astrobiologists even speculate that Titan's climate and chemistry are suitable for a different form of unearthly life. Instead of DNA, this form of life could be built on different molecules. For example, the alien molecules could have silicon atoms where Earth DNA has carbon atoms. Someday, scientists may send another probe to Titan to test this idea.

chapter 5

Galaxies of Life?

If you hope to find life somewhere in our solar system, astrobiologists will tell you to look for something simple, such as a microbe. But are you looking for complex life, such as plants and animals? Then you need to look beyond our solar system to other stars.

With so many stars in the Milky Way Galaxy, there are plenty of other solar systems. Some of them probably have planets as full of life as Earth. Some might even have civilizations with astrobiologists looking for life like their own. The big questions—for them and for us—are what to look for and where in the sky to look for it.

Are You There, Goldilocks?

Like Earth, our imaginary Goldilocks's home planet would have complex life. And it would have had this complex life for a long time before intelligent beings evolved. Then it would have taken even longer for those beings to develop a civilization—cities, centers for learning, and government. But if that civilization existed, it might be fairly easy for us to find it. That is the idea behind a part of astrobiology known as the Search for Extraterrestrial Intelligence (SETI).

Our best telescopes are not yet powerful enough to get a good look at the planets surrounding other stars. And we don't yet have technology to send spacecraft to another solar system. But the universe is filled with natural radio signals. Astronomers have built giant radio dishes to detect them. SETI researchers monitor those signals to look for artificial patterns. An artificial pattern might show that intelligent beings are sending the signals.

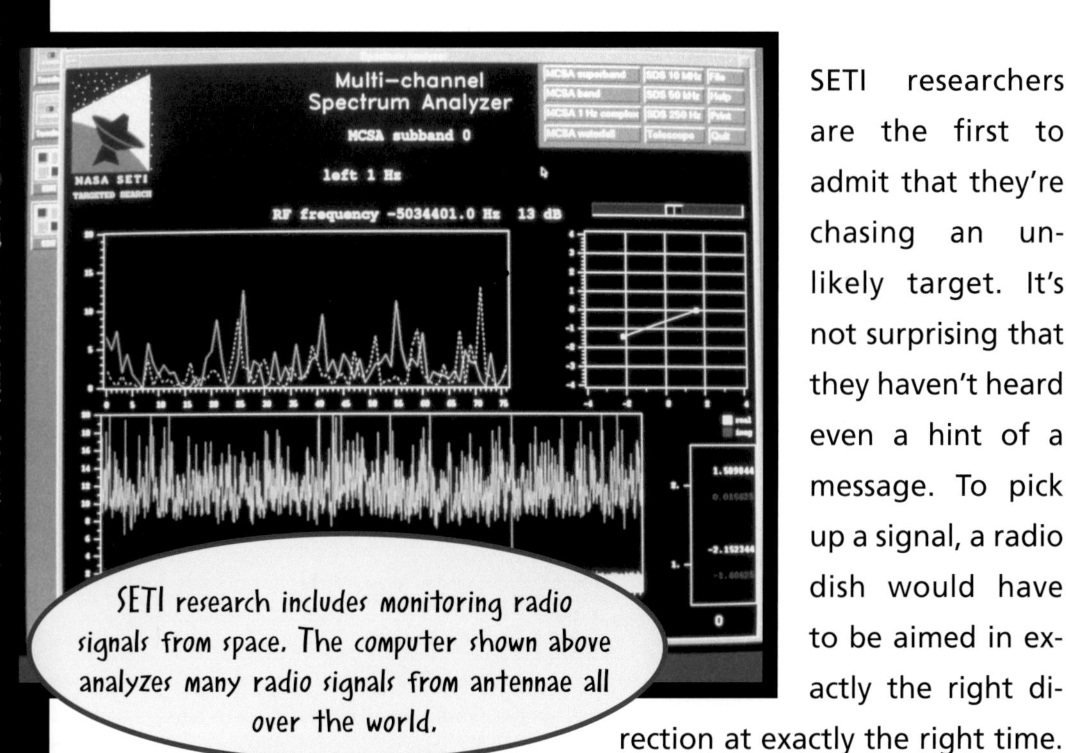

SETI research includes monitoring radio signals from space. The computer shown above analyzes many radio signals from antennae all over the world.

SETI researchers are the first to admit that they're chasing an unlikely target. It's not surprising that they haven't heard even a hint of a message. To pick up a signal, a radio dish would have to be aimed in exactly the right direction at exactly the right time. It would also have to be tuned to the frequency of the alien signal. But the task is not impossible. Astronomers are starting to find planets around many other stars. That gives SETI researchers a few good ideas of where to listen.

The Drake Equation

How did SETI research get started? In 1960 Frank Drake was a young astronomy professor at Cornell University in Ithaca, New York. He was the first scientist to search for signals from extraterrestrial civilizations. Drake's detector was a giant radio dish receiver at Green Bank, West Virginia. The next year, Drake organized the first scientific meeting on SETI at Green Bank. The scientists asked two questions. How many intelligent civilizations are likely in the Milky Way Galaxy? And how likely is it that we can find these civilizations?

To answer the conference's questions, the scientists came up with the Drake equation. The equation doesn't provide an exact answer that all astrobiologists can agree on. But by looking at the Drake equation term by term, we can see the many different questions modern astrobiologists are exploring.

In this photo from the early 1960s, Frank Drake (*left*) is shown working with other scientists at the National Radio Astronomy Observatory in Green Bank, West Virginia.

The equation begins with the number of stars in the Galaxy. That's the first step in guessing how many solar systems there could be. Astronomers don't know the number exactly. But they agree that the number of stars in our Milky Way Galaxy is huge—probably around a trillion. That's a million times a million! But few of those stars are suited to supporting living worlds. Some burn out very quickly. Others are in parts

The Palomar Observatory (*below*) is in Southern California, on Palomar Mountain. The observatory has four large, very powerful telescopes. Astronomers use them to study the stars and events in outer space.

of the Galaxy filled with powerful streams of energy. Those streams would make life on any nearby planets impossible. Still, if only one star in a thousand is suitable, there are a billion candidates in the Milky Way.

The next step in the equation is estimating how many moons and planets around the average star could support life. Based on what we know about our solar system, a reasonable guess is that the average star has at least one world where life might arise. That means the Galaxy probably contains at least a billion potentially habitable (suitable for life) worlds.

Just because a world can support life, that doesn't mean that it does. The next term in the Drake equation tackles that issue. It asks, how likely is it for some kind of simple life to develop on a habitable planet? Astrobiologists usually answer that all you need are enough of the right ingredients in the right place for life to begin. That is true even if starting life requires something so unusual that it happens on a planet only once in a million years. A million years seems very long to us. But the Galaxy is thousands of times older than that. Once-in-a-million-years events have happened thousands of times.

So most astrobiologists think that there are probably billions of worlds in the Galaxy where life has begun and probably still exists. Many of those worlds are in orbit around the Sun's closest neighboring stars.

A Place for Goldilocks

The next step in the Drake equation requires much more speculation. Not all astrobiologists agree on this step. It asks how likely it is for intelligent life to evolve from simple life. This question can be broken down into two parts. How likely is it for complex life to evolve from simple life? And how likely is it for complex life to evolve intelligence?

For answers, let's look at our own Goldilocks planet. Every species on Earth, including long-extinct plants and animals, have evolved and survived in places where the environment is just right. And that environment stayed just right for a long time.

The evolution of so many complex life-forms on Earth depends on a stable climate. Our climate has been stable for many thousands of years. This stability includes a regular cycle of seasons. Earth's seasons are caused by a tilt of its axis—the imaginary line that goes straight through Earth from the North Pole to the South Pole. Earth's axis keeps its direction steady as it revolves around the Sun over the course of the year. As long as Earth's tilt is steady, the cycle of seasons all over the planet is the same year after year.

Most planets don't have such a steady tilt. They spin like slightly off-balance toy tops. Their axes wobble and wander. Earth's axis would wander too, if it weren't for the Moon. Having such a large moon in orbit steadies Earth's axis. The Moon keeps the axis pointing in the same direction, just as a balancing pole makes it easier for a tightrope walker to stay upright. Without the stabilizing Moon, the pattern of Earth's seasons would change rapidly.

So a Goldilocks planet probably needs a large moon. But is there anything else? It probably also needs a friendly giant like Jupiter in the outer part of its solar system. That giant's powerful gravity could capture comets and other large bodies before they hit the Goldilocks planet. Astrobiologists figure that without Jupiter, large comets would have hit the young Earth frequently. Those impacts would have changed Earth's environment enough that complex life could never have developed.

More Questions

The next questions are these: Does complex life naturally develop into human-level intelligence—intelligence that includes the ability to communicate complex ideas? And if it develops that level of intelligence, will it develop technology to communicate across the Galaxy? Scientists know that several things led to the evolution of human intelligence. But is higher intelligence always a part of evolution? Some scientists say yes. Any planet that produces complex life will sooner or later produce intelligent life. Other scientists disagree. They argue that creatures only need to be smart enough to survive in their environment. It is not a rule of evolution that one or more species in a world would develop higher intelligence.

Still others argue that a creature smart enough to send radio signals into space might decide not to do so. Or worse, a species might get too smart for its own good. The human ability for communication and technology has produced many good things. But we have also developed weapons that can cause great destruction. We are also seeing signs that our technology may be changing the world's climate in a dangerous way. Will we be smart enough to deal with that?

The Drake Equation

Astrobiologists use the Drake equation to estimate the possibility of contacting intelligent alien civilizations. The equation looks like this:

$$N = R^* \times f_p \times n_e \times f_l \times f_i \times f_c \times L$$

N is the number of civilizations we could expect to communicate with. Each factor (letter) in the equation represents a step in figuring out that number. For example, the equation begins with R^*, the number of stars that form in the Milky Way Galaxy each year.

The other factors in the equation ask questions such as: How many of a star's planets and moons might support life? On how many of those worlds does life actually arise? On a planet where simple life is possible, how likely is it that complex life will evolve?

The last two terms of the equation describe the difference between complex life and life with humanlike intelligence. How likely is it that complex life will develop civilization and communications that can be detected on distant worlds? And how many years will that communicating civilization last?

Astrobiologists do not agree on all the terms. For example, one astrobiologist might think there is a 100 percent chance that life will develop on a Goldilocks planet. Another astrobiologist might think there is a much smaller chance.

Hopeful SETI scientists might think that one solar system in a hundred has a Goldilocks planet. Then they might think that one in a hundred Goldilocks planets develops high intelligence and sends messages into space. From that, they would calculate that thousands of message-sending worlds might develop in this galaxy. Less hopeful SETI researchers might conclude that the number is only a few. But whether there are many or a few, we could detect them—if we happen to be listening at the right time.

And that brings us to the final piece of the Drake equation. How long does a civilization last? Could a civilization last as long as its planet can support life? If the civilization is around for a long time, SETI will have a good chance of detecting its radio signals. But if an alien civilization destroys itself quickly, SETI would not have much of a chance to find it.

Humans first began producing radio signals about one hundred years ago. Our solar system has existed fifty million times as long. It's too soon to tell how smart we really are. We can only hope that we are smart enough and last long enough for that alien Goldilocks to find us—or for us to find her. Then we can study astrobiology together.

The radio telescope (*above*) at the Arecibo Observatory in Puerto Rico picks up signals from space. It is the world's most sensitive radio telescope. Its aluminum dish is 1,000 feet (305 m) in diameter. It rests in the Puerto Rican jungle.

Glossary

amino acid: a molecule that is one of the basic building blocks of proteins. Life on Earth is made of twenty different amino acids.

asteroid: a rocky body, smaller than a planet, in orbit around the Sun

astrobiologist: a scientist who studies life in the universe

atmosphere: the gases that form the outer layer of Earth or of an astronomical object

atom: a basic building block of matter. Atoms join together to form molecules.

bacteria: a class of very small life-forms on Earth made up of single cells

comet: a dusty, icy body that orbits the Sun

complex life: organisms that are made up of many cells and have internal organs and structures

deoxyribonucleic acid (DNA): the complex molecule that is the basis for all known life on Earth

evolution: a process by which life-forms change and new species come into being

galaxy: a large grouping of billions of stars, such as the Milky Way

gravity: a force that draws two objects together. On Earth it is the force that gives us weight and makes objects fall. It also keeps objects in orbit around one another.

intelligent life: complex life that has developed the ability to think

meteorite: a rocky or metallic object that has fallen to Earth from space

microbe: a living organism too small to be seen without a microscope

Milky Way Galaxy: the Galaxy that contains our Sun and the solar system

molecule: the smallest piece of a substance that can be recognized as that substance. Each molecule of the same kind is made of atoms in a particular combination.

moon: a major body that orbits a planet, such as the Moon that orbits Earth, Europa that orbits Jupiter, and Titan that orbits Saturn. A planet may have many moons.

orbit: the path followed by a smaller object under the influence of the gravity of a larger one

organism: a living being of any kind

planet: a large body that travels around a star

protein: a type of large, complex molecule, built from amino acids, that is the main substance in the organs of complex life-forms

solar system: the Sun and all the objects in orbit around it, including the planets and their moons, asteroids, comets, and other bodies. Other solar systems exist in the Milky Way and other galaxies, consisting of stars and orbiting objects.

speculation: a form of scientific thought based on ideas that are possible but unproven and even unlikely

Selected Bibliography

Basalla, George. *Civilized Life in the Universe: Scientists on Extraterrestrial Intelligence*. New York: Oxford University Press, 2005.

Cassidy, William. *Meteorites, Ice, and Antarctica: A Personal Account*. New York: Cambridge University Press, 2003.

Cohen, Jack, and Ian Stewart. *What Does a Martian Look Like? The Science of Extraterrestrial Life*. New York: Wiley, 2002.

Croswell, Ken. *Planet Quest: The Epic Discovery of Alien Solar Systems*. New York: Harcourt Brace, 1997.

Dorminey, Bruce G. *Distant Wanderers: The Search for Planets Beyond the Solar System*. New York: Copernicus Books, 2001.

Fischer, Daniel. *Mission Jupiter: The Spectacular Journey of the Galileo Spacecraft.* New York: Copernicus Books, 2001.

Gilster, Paul. *Centauri Dreams: Imagining and Planning Interstellar Exploration*. New York: Copernicus Books, 2005.

Jakosky, Bruce. *The Search for Life on Other Planets*. New York: Cambridge University Press, 1998.

Lemonick, Michael D. *Other Worlds: The Search for Life in the Universe*. New York: Simon & Schuster, 1998.

Levy, David H. *Impact Jupiter: The Crash of Comet Shoemaker-Levy 9*. New York: Plenum, 1995.

McSween, Harry Y., Jr. *Fanfare for Earth: The Origin of Our Planet and Life*. New York: St. Martins Press, 1997.

Plaxco, Kevin W., and Michael Gross. *Astrobiology: A Brief Introduction.* Baltimore: Johns Hopkins University Press, 2006.

Shostak, Seth. *Sharing the Universe: Perspectives on Extraterrestrial Life*. Berkeley, CA: Berkeley Hills Press, 1998.

Ward, Peter. *Life as We Do Not Know It: The NASA Search for (and Synthesis of) Alien Life*. New York: Viking, 2005.

Ward, Peter D., and Donald Brownlee. *The Life and Death of Planet Earth: How the New Science of Astrobiology Charts the Ultimate Fate of Our World*. New York: Henry Holt, 2002.

———. *Rare Earth: Why Complex Life Is Uncommon in the Universe*. New York, Copernicus Books, 2000.

Further Reading and Websites

ANSMET: The Antarctic Search for Meteorites. http://geology.cwru.edu/~ansmet/index.html. This Case Western Reserve University website features the latest news about the ANSMET project, including researchers' weblogs.

Bell, Jim. *Postcards from Mars: The First Photographer on the Red Planet*. New York: Dutton, 2006. This book is for adults, but readers of all ages can appreciate the wonderful images that tell the story of *Spirit* and *Opportunity*. These two robot rovers were expected to last only a few months after landing on Mars in early 2003. The book details the rovers' first three years of exploration.

Bortz, Fred. *Martian Fossils on Earth? The Story of Meteorite ALH84001*. Brookfield, CT: Millbrook Press, 1997. This book tells about the discoveries inside a rock from Mars that fell to Earth. It describes exciting scientific questions and controversies over what that meteorite could tell us about life on another world.

Jackson, Ellen, and Nic Bishop. *Looking for Life in the Universe.* Boston: Houghton Mifflin, 2002. This book in the Scientists in the Field series follows the work of SETI scientist Dr. Jill Tartar, including many photographs of SETI researchers at work.

Koppes, Steven. *Killer Rocks from Outer Space.* Minneapolis: Twenty-First Century Books, 2004. This book explores the catastrophic effects asteroids, comets, and meteorites had on early Earth.

NASA Astrobiology Institute. http://www.nai.arc.nasa.gov/. This is the central website for all NASA's research in astrobiology. It is mainly for adults, but young readers with a strong scientific interest in life on other worlds can discover the latest research news.

NASA Jet Propulsion Laboratory. http://www2.jpl.nasa.gov/snc/. This is the Mars meteorite home page, where adults and young readers can follow the latest discoveries about Meteorite ALH84001 and other pieces of Mars on Earth.

SETI Institute. http://www.seti.org/. The SETI Institute's home page has links to articles and information about the search for extraterrestrial intelligence. It is primarily for adults, but interested young visitors are welcome to explore.

Ward, D. J. *Exploring Mars*. Minneapolis: Lerner Publishing Company, 2007. In this volume of the Cool Science series, Ward looks at the Red Planet's physical characteristics. He examines our long-standing fascination with Mars and our most recent attempts to explore its surface.

Winner, Cherie. *Life on the Edge*. Minneapolis: Lerner Publishing Company, 2006. This book in the Cool Science series tells the stories and the science of extremophiles, creatures that thrive in extreme conditions on Earth. Astrobiologists study extremophiles as examples of life-forms that might dwell on Mars or other non-Goldilocks planets.

Index

Photo Acknowledgments

The images in the book are used with the permission of: NASA/JPL-Caltech/Harvard-Smithsonian CfA/ESA/STScI, pp. 1, all page backgrounds; NASA/JSC, p. 5; The Granger Collection, New York, p. 6; © Bruno Vincent/Getty Images, p. 7; © Hulton Archive/Getty Images, p. 9 (both); NASA and the Hubble Heritage Team (STScI/AURA) Acknowledgement: J. Bell (Cornell U.), P. James (U. Toledo), M. Wolff (Space Science Institute), A. Lubenow (STScI), J. Neubert (MIT/Cornell), p. 10 (top); © Bettmann/CORBIS, p. 10 (bottom); © Detlev van Ravenswaay/Photo Researchers, Inc., p. 11; Library of Congress, p. 12 (LC-USZ62-121026); NASA/JPL, pp. 15 (both), 26, 31; NASA/AMLAMP, p. 16; NASA/ARC, p. 19 (both); © Wolfgang Baumeister/Photo Researchers, Inc., p. 20 (left); © Eye of Science/Photo Researchers, Inc., p. 20 (right); Comstock Images, p. 21 (all); © Atlantide Phototravel/CORBIS, p. 24; NASA/JPL/MSSS, p. 27; NASA/JPL/Cornell, p. 28 (bottom); NASA/JPL/Cornell University/Maas Digital, p. 28 (inset); NASA/JPL/University of Arizona, p. 30; NASA/JPL/Space Science Institute, p. 32 (both); © SETI Institute/Photo Researchers, Inc., p. 35; © Michael Rougier/Time & Life Pictures/Getty Images, p. 36; © Chris Cook/Photo Researchers, Inc., p. 37; © David Parker/Photo Researchers, Inc., p. 41.

Front cover: NASA/JWST (top), PhotoDisc Royalty Free by Getty Images (middle), NASA/JPL-Caltech (bottom), NASA/JPL-Caltech/Harvard-Smithsonian CfA/ESA/STScI (background).

About the Author

Fred Bortz is a scientist and writer of science and technology for young people. In his books, articles, and personal appearances, he shares with his audience the joy of discovery that fueled his previous twenty-five-year career in teaching and research in physics, engineering, and science education. From 1979 through 1994, he was involved in research at Carnegie Mellon University, from which he earned his doctorate in physics in 1971. He is also a regular reviewer of science books for several major metropolitan newspapers.